PREPARING FOR YOUR INTERVIEW

Diane Berk

CRISP PUBLICATIONS, INC.
Los Altos, California

PREPARING FOR YOUR INTERVIEW

Diane Berk

CREDITS
Editor: **Elaine Brett**
Designer: **Carol Harris**
Typesetting: **Interface Studio**
Cover Design: **Carol Harris**
Artwork: **Ralph Mapson**

Copyright © 1990 by Crisp Publications, Inc.
Printed in the United States of America

Crisp books are distributed in Canada by Reid Publishing, Ltd., P.O. Box 7267, Oakville, Ontario, Canada L6J 6L6.

In Australia by Career Builders, P.O. Box 1051 Springwood, Brisbane, Queensland, Australia 4127.

And in New Zealand by Career Builders, P.O. Box 571, Manurewa, New Zealand.

Library of Congress Catalog Card Number 89-82098
Berk, Diane
Preparing for your Interview
ISBN 1-56052-033-7

CONTENTS

INTRODUCTION

You're excited about an upcoming interview. Everything you've heard about the job—including the salary, benefits, hours, and location—sounds ideal. Best of all, you know you've got the perfect qualifications. And so, with boundless confidence, you go in, give it your all and. . .get a rejection letter!

Obviously, the interview didn't go as well as it could have. Your qualifications were right, but so were those of the other applicants interviewed. Perhaps the one who got the job had a firmer handshake or answered tough questions with greater ease.

When qualifications *are* equal, it's incumbent on you to stand out by being the best interviewee. Fortunately, this is a skill that can be learned.

This is a concise guide designed to prepare you for job hunting. You can read through it once or refer to it each time you're going on an interview for quick reminders and pointers. I suggest reading over the ''do's and don'ts'' before to each interview.

As a corporate recruiter and personnel manager, I've interviewed hundreds of individuals for a wide variety of positions and have seen many of them ask the wrong questions, look nervous, and seem to be unprepared. *Preparing for Your Interview* was designed to give you an experienced interviewer's insider knowledge so that you can avoid mistakes.

Of course, you'll still need to meet the requirements for the position. But the information in this guide will give you an extra edge over your competition and increase your chances of getting the job you want.

Good luck!

TYPES OF INTERVIEWS

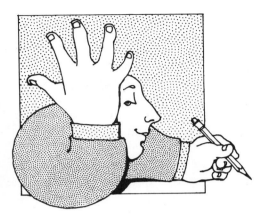

An interview gives the applicant and the interviewer an opportunity to exchange information that's relevant to the position at hand. Some interviewers are skilled at eliciting detailed personal information, while others are content to "merely scratch" the surface. If at all possible, find out what type of interview you're going to have, since you will need to prepare accordingly. Sometimes you won't know ahead of time what type of interview it will be, so you'll have to evaluate it while it's progressing and determine what information to provide and what questions are appropriate to ask.

Interviews can be classified into five types: *screening, selection, group, serial,* and *exploratory* (though these are occasionally known by different names). Each type will be defined and the information and advice given in this book will be differentiated when it is more suitable for one type of interview than another.

The Screening Interview

In screening interviews, inappropriate applicants are "screened out" from becoming potential candidates. You can consider these interviews to be preliminary discussions and expect that many applicants will not be called back for a second interview. Your best approach is to consider it to be a screening interview from your side as well. This means that you will ask only general questions about the position and company. It is acceptable to ask what the salary range is at a screening interview, but detailed salary negotiation is not done until the selection interview, described next. Interviewers should always answer all your questions (even when they've made up their minds that you're not right for the job), so if you really want to know more, *ask.*

Remember that the interviewer may get impatient thinking about all the other applicants waiting in the reception area. If you sense that the interviewer is trying to hurry you along, it's probably a bad idea to push and continue asking questions. The time to ask more questions is during the selection interview.

The Selection Interview

This is the critical interview during which the employer will evaluate your work and school history, your determination and goals, what motivates you, your potential, and so on. While some of the more concrete elements such as school and work history can be presented on paper, the interviewer's perception of your personality traits will be determined by what you say and do. In other words, the selection interview is your chance to shine and the employer's chance to make decisions about you. It will be the most detailed and in-depth interview you have.

The selection interview can be conducted by either a recruiter or another employee of the employment department or by the manager of the department in which you're hoping to work. Whoever does the interviewing, expect this type of interview to be probing and wide-ranging.

You are now a viable candidate for the position, being compared against other applicants with similar backgrounds. This is your opportunity to impress the interviewer with the quality of your questions and your comments about the company so that you'll stand out among the group of candidates (assuming you have equal qualifications). This will also be the time to ask about the goals of the company and department, the company's philosophy, the job description and how it might be enhanced, and other key issues. You might be asked about your attitude regarding specific work situations and how you relate to co-workers and supervisors, and you may also be asked to state your personal long-term goals.

This is the interview during which salary and benefits are usually discussed. This is not a fixed rule, however. This topic may be mentioned in a more general way in the screening interview as well.

It is important that both you and your interviewer leave this meeting feeling that everything was said that needed to be said and that you both have all the information you need to make a decision.

The Group Interview

For some individuals, a group interview is the most frightening meeting imaginable. With one interviewer, you can concentrate on making eye contact, getting comfortable, and making small talk. When you are interviewed by three, five, or even more people, you'll constantly be aware of all those eyes watching you as you speak, which may make you more self-conscious about what you're saying and how you're saying it.

If you're going to be meeting with a group of people, you'll probably be told ahead of time by a representative of the company. This will give you time to prepare mentally for it. You will prepare just as you would for any other interview, but with the knowledge that you may not be asked questions in a logical sequence as you would if you were with one individual. The questions and comments may be unrelated to each other, which can easily derail your train of concentration. Another problem is that, while you may get signs of encouragement with one interviewer, with a group you may get what seem to be signs of uncertainty and indifference.

Group interviews are conducted partly to see how candidates react under the pressure of talking to several personalities, to see how well honed their social skills are, or to see whether they would fit in with the group. Usually group interviews are conducted by a group of individuals from the department that has the opening you are applying for. These people are the very ones with whom you will work if you get the job, and one of the primary goals is to see how well you would blend with these potential co-workers.

Group interviews are often conducted during lunch, and you may be taken out to a restaurant by two or more people. This is not to be considered time off, though. You may be asked many of the same questions you would have been asked back in the conference room, only in a more relaxed atmosphere. Nevertheless, don't interpret the friendly lunch as a time to change your behavior or discuss inappropriate personal issues. Remember that you're being evaluated at all times.

> ◆**TIP:** When you're being introduced to everyone, try very hard to hear and remember their names. Try associating the individual with someone else you know by the same name, or rhyme their name with something in your mind. It is impressive when you can turn to someone and use his or her name rather than asking, ''What is your name again, please?'' Having to ask will leave the impression that you were too nervous when you arrived to really concentrate.

Serial Interviews

This is simply a series of interviews of varying types with various people. It may start with a screening interview with a recruiter in the human resources department and move on to a selection interview with the vice president of that division. You might then be sent on to the supervisor of the department in which you hope to work. You may be asked to meet some of the people or a group of people from other departments you'd work with. Some companies set up an impressive series of interviews for final candidates for key positions.

The important thing to remember is that you may be asked the same questions over and over. Each person will think their question is very original, however. You must therefore remain fresh and stimulating throughout the entire process and make each meeting seem like it's your first. This may be tough if it's been a long day, but it's extremely important to engage each interviewer equally.

Exploratory Interviews

An exploratory interview is somewhat the opposite of a screening interview in that the applicant sets up the interview to screen that company as a potential place to work.

Many people who want to move ahead or find out about a new field or career call potential employers to ask whether someone there would be willing to meet with them on an exploratory basis. This is one of the best ways to find a position, even though nothing may be open at the time of the interview. Job seekers try to leave a lasting positive impression with the company so that when something *does* open up, they'll be remembered.

You'll definitely need to do your homework if you're going in for an exploratory interview. You'll need to ask a wide range of questions about the company and the types of positions available. You will be taking up the time of someone who agreed to see you when no openings are currently available. You can't expect that person to keep the conversation going when you're the one who asked for the meeting in the first place.

To make a lasting impression, you should be prepared to ask a variety of questions and to leave your most current resume behind. You also want to convey as much positive information as you can and create a favorable overall impression. No matter how impressive you are, however, don't be surprised if the interviewer starts acting impatient. Once you sense you are taking up too much of that person's time, wind up what you have to say and thank him or her for the meeting.

> ♦TIP: If you're with someone who is getting edgy, ask questions about him or her. People love to talk about themselves and are usually more than willing to do so. It's a form of flattery to ask how they got started in the industry or how they got hired by the company. In this way, you might find that your exploratory interview will last longer and you'll leave more of a lasting impression.

Telephone Interviews

Occasionally a recruiter conducts an interview by telephone. Two common situations in which this occurs: when a national company is hiring for a regional office or when the applicant is being recruited from another city and can't leave home for an interview. Rather than fly across the country, the recruiter arranges to meet the applicant on the telephone.

Telephone interviews are not the optimum method of interviewing for either party. In particular, the applicant has no opportunity to display personality traits through dress and body language. It's difficult for some people to convey their personal flair through a phone conversation.

It's ironic that some people may consider a telephone interview a *plus* for these very same reasons, because they are understandably relieved to be judged solely on merit and job experience and not on their looks, mannerisms, or choice of clothing.

Treat a telephone interview as you would any other. Take it seriously, because interviewers will be making an evaluation of you based on whatever information and impressions they can gather.

Despite the distinctions made here between different types of interviews, bear in mind that they often overlap and that you may not know in advance precisely what to expect. Prepare as best you can for the type of interview you are anticipating, but be ready to switch strategic gears in midstream if necessary.

For example, you may believe you are going to be given a brief screening interview. However, if you say something that leads the interviewer to believe you have unusually good qualifications, he or she may shift into a more in-depth, selection-type interview. Follow your interviewer's lead and exchange detailed information along the way.

RESEARCH

Few job seekers realize how important a little investigation can be prior to an interview. If you come into an interview armed with information about the company, you'll be able to ask intelligent questions and supply specifics about how you can benefit that company. It will also leave the impression that you are both savvy and willing to take initiative.

There are different ways to obtain useful information. If it's a large corporation, familiarize yourself with its products or services. Many corporations have brochures and publicity material available to the public. Use the reference desk of your public library to find articles that have been written in newspapers and magazines. For current financial information, try to obtain an annual report. This may also outline a company's goals for the next year.

Try to talk to an employee or former employee of the company. You can learn a lot from this person, but remember that what you're told may well be colored by his or her own (possibly negative) experiences.

Collect information that gives you a sense of the company's goals and identity, and that will prompt you to ask pertinent questions during the interview. These questions can cover everything from the background of the company to its plans for the coming years. These should always be general questions about the company, not ones that relate to you personally. Those will come later.

Your goal is to impress the interviewer with your questions and with the quality of your homework. You will have displayed your eagerness and shown that you're not just there to see what the company can offer you, but also how your skills and interests may benefit the company.

RESEARCH INFORMATION

The following questions will help find out about a company when you're doing research. Fill in the blanks as you acquire information.

What is the product produced or the service offered by the company? _____

_____

Where is the product or service sold and to whom? _____

_____

How many years has the company been in business? _____

_____

How has the focus of the company shifted since its inception? _____

_____

Has management been fairly stable or has there been excessive turnover?

_____

Is the company publicly or privately owned? _____

_____

Has the stock remained stable and strong or does it fluctuate often? What affects the stock prices? _____

_____

Have there been any takeover attempts of the company? _____

_____

Is realizing a profit affected by intangible forces such as weather or politics?

_____

Is the product or service seasonal? Are employees hired accordingly? _____

_____

Has the company realized a profit from the product or service in the last year? In the last five years? _____

_____

Has the company laid off employees in the last three years? Why? _____

_____

Is the company part of a conglomerate? _____

_____

Is the company highlighted in the press? Why? Is it positive or negative press?

_____

Is the company known for its innovative treatment toward employees?

_____

Is the company known for its conservative treatment toward employees?

_____

Is the company unionized? Which union? How strong is the union? _____

_____

What new ventures is the company planning to undertake? _____

_____

Is the company based solely in the United States or does it have offices and interests abroad? _____

_____

Is the company part of a growing industry? _____

_____

What are the projections for the industry? _____

_____

SETTING UP THE INTERVIEW

Interviews are often arranged by the assistant or secretary of the person with whom you'll be meeting. It's of the utmost importance that you treat this person with respect and courtesy. Smart managers pay attention when their assistant says, ''Boy, was that guy rude!'' You'll have one strike against you if that happens.

While you're on the phone making arrangements, ask for directions and parking instructions. You don't want to be 15 minutes late because you couldn't find a parking space. It's also a good idea to ask whether you should bring a resume (although you should always have a few with you). For creative jobs, it's appropriate to ask whether you should bring samples of your work—writing samples or a portfolio, for example.

You may be secretly interviewing while you are already employed. This may limit your interviewing time to lunch breaks and evenings, unless you use the infamous appointment-with-the-dentist excuse.

If you *are* going to lie to your current boss, be prepared for any eventuality. What if your car breaks down or the train is late? What if the personnel director likes you so much that he or she decides to take you upstairs to meet the vice president of the department? You arrive back at your office three hours later with a mouthful of lame excuses instead of a mouthful of freshly cleaned teeth.

This is not the ideal condition in which to be interviewed, since your anxiety will almost certainly show. Try to arrange your interviews when you'll have all the time needed. Future employers will respect your conscientiousness if you explain that you can't leave your job for two hours without lying. You might suggest an after-work appointment or, if need be, take a day of vacation time.

Finally, always call to confirm your appointment at least eight hours in advance.

THE INTERVIEW

Once you've arrived (early) and greeted the receptionist (warmly), you may be given a lengthy application to complete. Since these are important to a company for both legal and record keeping purposes don't sneer at the receptionist and say, "I brought my resumé. Do I have to fill this out?" The answer is clear; do what they ask you to do.

Once you sit down with the interviewer or recruiter, chances are he or she will begin with small talk. This is meant to be an icebreaker and to give you a chance to regroup if you're nervous.

The hardest opening question to respond to is, "So, tell me about yourself." Begin by explaining why you're interested in the job or by describing your understanding of the position. You might say, "In the advertisement for this position, it stated that programming experience was helpful but not required. Why is this?" Or you might mention that while you were in college you worked for a company that produces a similar product. A focused response like this raises appropriate questions and sidesteps areas that have more to do with your personality than with your job qualifications.

The interviewer may (and *should*) begin with a more specific question about your experience or by describing the position or the company. Listen carefully. Let the interviewer guide the conversation because he or she has a definite agenda. You'll be anxious to provide positive information about yourself, but if you're busy rehearsing what you're going to say, you won't hear everything being said. Try to integrate what you want to say naturally into the conversation.

Your answers to questions should be direct and succinct. This doesn't mean a simple yes or no. (If you're with a savvy interviewer, you won't be able to answer any questions with yes or no anyway; more on this later.) *Direct* means answering the question that's asked, and *succinct* means staying within the confines of the subject being discussed.

For example, if the interviewer asks, "What were your special achievements while you were in college?" talk about those achievements, but *avoid* continuing to list the exemplary things you achieved at your last two positions. The interviewer may have a specific reason for asking about your college achievements and may have been planning to ask a follow-up question. By going beyond the sufficient answer, you may shift the conversation into an area that the interviewer was planning to move to later.

On the other hand, you can answer the question *and* provide information that will work in your favor. If, for example, you are asked what your responsibilities were in the advertising department, you could not only outline them but add that your efforts resulted in a 25% increase in newspaper placement over a six-month period. This would be seen as relevant information, and no one could think of you as being a braggart for having introduced it.

The interviewer usually directs the conversation but allows you to do most of the talking. If your interviewer seems to leave you with long stretches of silence, you may feel decidedly uncomfortable. In actuality, though, this is a technique used to urge you to say more and make you feel that you have all the time you need. It's *not* a ploy to get you off balance.

Telling the Truth

This next piece of advice will sound obvious and preachy: you should tell the truth. Everyone tends to exaggerate and embellish their experience during an interview and a little of this is expected. However, if you exaggerate or actually lie to the extent that what you're saying can't be substantiated, you'll get yourself in trouble in several ways.

First, you'll probably be more transparent than you realize. You may appear anxious or hesitant, which may give the interviewer doubts about you. Inevitably, each lie will provoke the now doubtful interviewer into asking you a follow-up question, and you'll only get in deeper and deeper.

Secondly, even if you're convincing *now*, you'll still need to deliver later when you start the job. Obviously, you could experience tremendous embarrassment if you've said you can do something that you really can't.

Finally, most applications state in small print that falsifying information can lead to immediate dismissal (that's assuming you lied well enough to get the job). Don't lie; it will come back to haunt you. Even if you are never caught, you'll always wonder whether someone will figure it out.

Preparing for Questions

It is impossible to prepare for every question that you'll be asked, but you can have an idea of how you'll answer general and often-asked questions. Read the sample questions that follow for a basic idea of what may be asked of you. A word of caution, however: don't memorize answers to these questions. Your interviewer might have very different questions that are specific to the position. You can prepare by thinking, "If I'm asked these questions, how will I answer?" But don't have the responses to every anticipated question rehearsed as if you're reading from a script.

> ◆**TIP:** There are some answers that seasoned interviewers have heard a million times: for example, "I'm a people person" or "I want to work somewhere where there is opportunity for growth." These statements may be true, but you need to convey the meaning in a more original, less cliché-ridden way. Offer an example that illustrates *how* you acted as a "people person" by listening more constructively to customers or by forming a cooperative work group. Or demonstrate *how* you've taken advantage of growth opportunities in the past by taking on extra projects that gave you new skills. Your interviewer will be more impressed if you avoid overused, trite statements.

SAMPLE QUESTIONS

This sampling of standard questions an interviewer may ask you can be used to prepare for an interview, but remember *not* to memorize your responses, since you may be asked a totally different set of questions. Use these as a general guide to the basic types of questions recruiters and managers are taught to ask, and to think about possible answers you might give.

1. Why did you select the major you did in college? _____

_____

2. What are your prime responsibilities in your current job? _____

_____

3. How do you spend your average work day? _____

_____

4. How do you prioritize your workload? _____

_____

5. What aspect of your job do you enjoy the most and least? _____

_____

6. What problems do you encounter in your job? _____

_____

7. What tends to frustrate you? _____

_____

8. What do you find challenging? _____

_____

9. Why are you considering leaving your present position? _____

_____

10. Why did you leave your last job? _____
_____

11. Why were you laid off? Discharged? _____
_____

12. In what ways has or hasn't your supervisor developed your skills? _____
_____

13. What types of things did you and your supervisor disagree and agree on?
_____

14. How was your performance evaluated? _____
_____

15. How did you respond to your evaluation? _____
_____

16. Ideally, what would you hope to find in a job and company? _____
_____

17. What goals would you like to achieve in one year? Five? _____
_____

18. What do you think best qualifies you for this position? _____
_____

19. How does this job fit into your overall career objectives? _____
_____

20. How could you make a difference to this company? _____
_____

Explaining Negative Situations

When you talk about past negative experiences, you may inadvertently display attitudes that will raise warning signals for your interviewer. You may harbor a negative attitude toward your former employer or supervisor, for example, but don't be *so* honest in an interview that you reveal all your pent-up bitterness or hostility.

Perhaps you and your former supervisor had a noticeable personality conflict that eventually led you to quit. If you say this, though, your interviewer may surmise that you are prone to interpersonal problems and be leary of hiring you even if your qualifications are rock solid.

You need to be truthful about why you quit the job, yet at the same time you don't want to create an unfair strike against yourself in the process. What, then, is your best course of action? Give your side of the story in precise details, rather than in emotional generalities. Avoid vague comments like, "He (or she) just had it in for me from the start." Explain specific areas in which you and your supervisor disagreed and examples of situations in which your ideas weren't used. You can describe how accessible you made yourself with no reciprocation from your supervisor, the accomplishments you had with little or no recognition, and so on. You need to give tangible and reasonable explanations for your leaving (or being laid off or terminated), without revealing your resentment. To sound truly mature and balanced, give the other side of the story as well. If you look beyond your hurt feelings, you may find the reasons your supervisor felt the way he or she did.

Explaining why you were terminated (a nicer way of saying fired) is rarely a comfortable process. Be candid while walking the fine line of not doing more damage to yourself as an applicant.

Some applicants have negative feelings not only towards their former employers, but towards the interviewer. If you're an attorney, you may feel it's ridiculous for the personnel manager to screen you before anyone in the legal department does. You may convey an attitude of indifference to the interviewer's evaluation because you assume that the personnel manager knows very little about the legal profession. Naturally, that person will be left with a negative impression and your potential career with the company might already be over. Be sure to put all of your prejudices aside *before* your meeting.

Anxiety is another emotion that interferes with successful interviewing. We're not talking about nervousness; interviewers see many good candidates who are nervous. The anxiety in this instance occurs when someone literally is overly anxious to land the job. Unemployed people who are frightened by their situation may say things like, ''I'll do anything!'' However, since this will not be interpreted as dedication, but rather as desperation, definitely it is not a good strategy.

If you truly *are* desperate and *will* do anything, at least make an attempt to carefully screen the jobs and companies you're looking at.

♦**TIP:** Consider applying for temporary, part-time work to support yourself while you search for a job tailormade for you. Many great job offers have come out of temporary jobs.

To summarize, your interview will be directed by the person with whom you are meeting, since they'll know exactly what they want to learn about you. It's essential that you tell them the truth about your background and that you explain negative events in an honest, balanced way. Prepare yourself to a reasonable extent, but expect to answer questions for which you're unprepared. Above all else, relax!

WHO ARE RECRUITERS?

Professional interviewers are trained to learn a great deal about you in a short time, while you get to know very little about them. Of course, there's generally no real reason for you to get to know these people, but it may help to understand a bit about recruiting as a profession.

A recruiter must be a spokesperson, judge, and salesperson all at the same time. Recruiters are hired in large part for their communication skills and ability to handle several situations at once. They are often people who are interested in moving up the ladder in the field of human resources and see recruitment as a stepping-stone. Inasmuch as they'll be evaluated on the successful placements they make, they clearly need you as much as you need them. Generally, recruiters (compared to department supervisors and managers) see applicants for screening interviews.

Recruiters have been trained in varying degrees, ranging from three-day seminars to lengthy, in-depth courses. Some have no formal training at all. Their most important task is to learn about each of the positions to be filled so they can assess résumés and conduct interviews fairly. Only rarely do recruiters have personal experience in the position for which you're interviewing.

Do not conclude that this interview won't matter and that it's a waste of your time. Recruiters screen out the best applicants and recommend them to managers. Occasionally, they even make hiring decisions on their own. They are to be taken very seriously and so should you in your interview with them.

Recruiters see many people during screening interviews, so your interview may be short and less intense than subsequent ones. Expect a more in-depth interview from the director of personnel or the manager of a department who hasn't spent most of his or her day interviewing candidates.

Although later interviews by managers may be more in-depth, the interviewer will likely be less trained. In many large companies, management spends time and money training all managers in basic human resource-oriented topics such as interviewing skills. In companies like this, your interviews are likely to be well directed, focused, informative, and open. Unfortunately, most managers do not have special training in interviewing skills, and people you meet outside the personnel department may not conduct interviews in which the information exchanged is consistently useful.

INTERVIEWING TECHNIQUES

What follows are descriptions of techniques commonly used by trained managers and recruiters in most companies. You will be more comfortable in your interview if you understand why the interviewer is asking you questions in a certain fashion. Trained interviewers have learned some or all of the techniques that follow.

Explaining the Agenda

By first mapping out what will be covered in the interview, the interviewer will be giving you a chance to relax. You'll know what's coming, what your time limits will be (although they should always be flexible), and what topics you'll need to bring up.

Open-Ended Questions

These are questions that can't be answered with a ''yes'' or ''no.'' So, instead of asking, ''Were you always on time to work?'' they'll ask, ''What type of work habits are important to you?'' This forces you to say more and allows the interviewer to say less. It is a basic rule of thumb for effective interviewing to avoid yes/no questions.

General Questions

An astute applicant will have pat answers to questions such as, ''What is your five-year goal?'' or ''Why did you choose the major you did?'' An experienced interviewer attempts to ask more specific questions or to rephrase general questions so that the applicant can't fall back on rehearsed answers.

Leading Questions

It is possible for interviewers to set you up to succeed by phrasing questions so that they lead you to give the "right" answers. This is a tactic that interviewers should use very rarely.

Neutral Questions

Effective interviewers know they should never reveal their attitudes about anything by the way they phrase their questions and comments.

Encouragement

Rather than quickly continuing on to the next question, good interviewers encourage an applicant to expand on the last answer. This can be done nonverbally with subtle gestures such as a nod of the head or with phrases such as "Go on," and "How interesting."

Silence

Good interviewers also give you time to respond and do not ask more questions before you finish answering the last one. For example, if the interviewer asks you what task you enjoyed most in your last job, he or she shouldn't jump in with, "Was it entering data on your PC?" It's *your* interview and you should be answering the questions.

Interviewers often remain silent even when you're not speaking. As mentioned, silence is terribly awkward for some people, but it isn't designed to make you nervous. It's the interviewer's job to listen very carefully to everything you say and to absorb the information. Silence is needed to think about what you've just said and decide whether a follow-up question is necessary. Try your best not to let a few seconds of silence here and there make you uncomfortable, because it's an important facet of an effective interview.

BODY LANGUAGE AND DRESS

Your mind will probably be racing as you anticipate what you'll say and how you'll behave, but the first impression you create will be visual and the importance of body language, grooming, and dress can't be overestimated.

When you research a company, you might learn that its policies are particularly conservative or that the prevailing attitude is extremely casual. *Whatever* you discover, a good rule of thumb is to overdress and lean toward the conservative. If it turns out that jeans and T-shirts are standard there, you can dress the part once you have the job.

Men should wear a suit and tie. The suit doesn't have to be dark, three-piece, or pinstriped, but it should be somewhat conservative in color and style. Naturally, there are situations where only a *very* conservative suit is appropriate, such as in interviews at financial institutions or law firms. On the other hand, if you're interviewing with a design or record company, it may be more suitable to interview in a sport jacket and trendy tie.

Women have more choices in dress and therefore can make more mistakes. Suits and conservative dresses are the best bet for women as well; avoid extremes in length, color, and frills. The more staid the company, the more conservative the outfit should be. You can personalize your clothes with tasteful understated jewelry and accessories. Stay away from pants, miniskirts, sweaters, and anything that's overly trendy or casual.

◆**TIP:** Interviews are an ideal time to make a mental note of how employees dress on the job, so that you'll be sure to look professional by dressing the part when you are—hopefully—an employee yourself.

A firm handshake makes a tremendous impression on an interviewer, but it always takes him or her a few moments to concentrate after shaking a clammy, limp hand. Make sure your hand is dry, even if it means wiping it inconspicuously on your clothes or hiding a napkin in your pocket.

A firm handshake accompanied by a genuine smile and direct eye contact sets a positive tone. The interviewer gets the nonverbal message that this is a straightforward, confident person.

You should appear calm and comfortable, whatever your internal thoughts. Sit in natural positions, bearing in mind that you're not on your own couch at home. Avoid crossing your arms tightly across your chest, because this is often perceived as an indication that you close people out.

Make eye contact throughout your meeting. If you're nervous and have an inclination to look down, try to catch yourself and look at your interviewer.

Many people have little nervous habits that they're unaware of. For that reason, you may want to try a few practice interviews with a friend. What do you unconsciously do when you're speaking? Do you pick at your nails? Play with your hair? Have your friend point out any such unwanted habits, and then find ways to avoid them. Fold your hands, wear your hair up—do *whatever* is necessary to make you appear cool and collected.

NEGOTIATING SALARY

Many people find this the most uncomfortable part of an interview, but it doesn't have to be that way. Just remember that this can be equally awkward for your interviewer, which means that you may be more emotionally in sync than you think.

Prepare for your interview with a few figures in mind: what you're currently making, what you would like to make, and the minimum you'll accept. While these aren't necessarily figures you'll end up agreeing on, they'll give you and the interviewer a base from which to work and serve to demonstrate how prepared you are.

Salary is one of the last things that should be discussed and it's best brought up by the interviewer. If, early in the interview, you ask, ''What does this job pay?'' the answer may end up limiting you. A price will now have been named and you won't have had the opportunity to show why you're worth more.

If, on the other hand, the interviewer asks, ''What salary are you looking for?'' or ''Let's discuss remuneration,'' you will have a springboard from which to start. You can name a figure and emphasize the reasons why you feel you deserve that amount (without *over*-selling yourself or being completely immodest).

Unfortunately, you won't always have flexibility in negotiating salary. If you're a recent college graduate, you may not have a long salary history. Or you may be applying for a position in which the salary has little or no range. In situations such as these, you may have to decide whether you want the position enough to accept the figure offered. If instinct tells you there's no room for negotiation, don't push it.

Your research or prior history in a related job should give you an idea of what a given position should pay. Make sure you've done your homework, because it can be embarrassing to ask for a salary that's ridiculously higher (ten thousand or more) than the one being offered. Make sure you know what the market will bear.

Conversely, don't make the mistake of underevaluating yourself. Accepting a cut in pay will be expected if you're changing careers and starting at the bottom. But if you're looking for a position similar to one you once had or have now, you should make every effort to *increase* your salary. Prospective employers look at salary history as a clue to your success in past positions. They'll make the natural judgment that you must have done well to get the promotions and increases you did. Salary history will also be used as a clue to personality traits such as aggressiveness and negotiating skills. Accepting significantly less money may work against you for all of these reasons.

> ♦**TIP:** If you want a particular job so much that you're willing to take a cut in pay, you can try to make up the salary difference in other ways. Ask for three weeks of vacation rather than two, or negotiate a bonus system. Some people negotiate for overtime pay in positions where it wouldn't normally be paid or for "comp" days in exchange for overtime.

Interviewers assume that many applicants inflate their salary history. Misrepresentation isn't recommended, because prospective employers may go to great lengths to find out whether you've been truthful. If they think you're exaggerating, they may be less inclined to negotiate a higher salary for you. Once again, it's always prudent to be honest.

NEGOTIATING BENEFITS

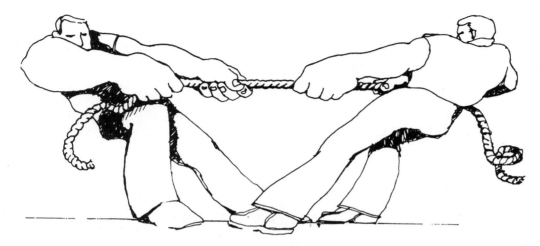

Like salary, you won't want to bring up benefits too early in the conversation. You may be perceived as someone who's far more interested in paid holidays than in the job itself.

The interviewer may broach the subject as he or she goes through an agenda of items to be discussed. If this is the case, you can integrate your questions into the conversation.

Be sure to ask more than simply whether medical benefits are offered. *Benefits* have come to mean a number of different things over the years. In their pursuit of hiring the best applicants, many companies have added more and more innovative benefits or "perks."

In today's competitive job market, the list can include:

- Medical insurance/HMO options
- Dental insurance
- Vision plan
- Prescription plan
- Life insurance/dependent life insurance
- 401K plan
- Retirement/pension plan
- Profit sharing
- Paid holidays
- Vacation days
- Sick pay
- Long and short-term disability
- Training programs (provided in-house or seminars that will be paid for)
- Management training
- Tuition reimbursement
- Child care
- Employee exercise facility
- Van pooling
- Flex days
- Paid parking

Only the most innovative companies would offer all of these benefits to employees. Most offer only medical and life insurance, sick pay, and vacation days; other benefits are considered too expensive.

Applicants' needs and preferences in the area of benefits vary, depending upon lifestyle and priorities. The key is to know what your priorities are before an interview so you can find out about those benefits that mean the most to you and your family.

> ◆**TIP:** Remember when you're discussing and negotiating benefits, ask who will *pay* for the benefits. Are they covered 100% by the employer, is dependent coverage paid for? If the benefits are going to cost *you* too much, you may need to negotiate further.

REFERENCES

Your skills and experience will have the most weight in the final evaluation of whether or not you're the best candidate for the job, but other pieces of information will additionally be important. One of these is your references.

There's no way of knowing how seriously a prospective employer considers references. Some conscientiously call everyone on your list, while others prefer to rely on their own intuitions.

References have become an area of legal debate over the last few years. It used to be as simple as giving names and phone numbers of former supervisors to your potential employer, who called them to ask questions about you. Things have changed, however, because slander and libel suits have been filed against former employers who gave negative information that hindered the former employee from getting a job.

As a result, most larger companies now have strict policies about providing references, usually insisting that calls to managers about former employees be directed to the personnel department. The spokesperson in that department may limit the information given to the dates of employment, the position held, and possible salary background. What *won't* be revealed is why the person in question is no longer employed. Smaller companies that aren't aware of the potential for lawsuits, though, may be inclined to offer information on *every* aspect of a former employee.

If you were a stellar employee, it can be frustrating to know that very little will be said about you. On the other hand, if you were ''terminated for cause,'' you can relax, knowing that your prospective employer might not hear about it.

You should know that this is not a black and white rule. There are large companies where managers *do* offer information because there is no policy regarding references. If you're staying within one industry and exploring a move to the competition, the prospective employer may hear of your plans simply by calling a colleague. This happens quite frequently and is out of your control. Hopefully, it will work to your advantage.

Prepare for the references game by finding out whether your current company has a policy regarding references, and what that policy is. What you learn may make you rethink who you'll give as references.

> ♦**TIP:** Prospective employers prefer professional over personal references because they're a better indicator of your success at work.

If it won't endanger your current job, let your references know you're going to give their names, so that they can jot down notes before being called. It might also be helpful if you tell them a little about the position you're applying for.

Bring the names, phone numbers, and addresses of your references with you to your interview so that you'll be prepared if the interviewer requests such information.

Some employers give candidates authorization forms giving them the go-ahead to procure references. This is usually just a simple form stating that the signature below (belonging to the applicant) authorizes them to answer the questions on the form. This is obviously a method of getting written references and usually the form is short and asks a few simple questions.

Most reference checks are done over the telephone. The caller asks a series of questions. The box on the facing page lists sample questions to give you an idea of the type of information sought.

Questions Often Asked in Reference Checks

Can you verify the dates the employee worked for your company?

What was the employee's job title?

Can you give a basic description of the job the employee had?

How would you rate the employee as a supervisor?

How did the employee respond to supervision?

Was the employee reliable, and on time? Were sick days excessive or kept to a minimum?

What was your working relationship with the employee?

Are there any negative aspects of the employee that stand out?

What positive attributes stand out?

Can you verify the employee's salary?

Is the employee eligible for rehire with your company?

Did the employee receive raises or promotions while with your company?

Did the employee display initiative?

How did the employee interact with peers?

What is your overall impression of the employee?

If the employee's former company has a strict policy regarding references, the questions will be limited to:

Can you verify that (name) worked for your company?

Can you verify his or her salary?

Employees sometimes try to get around giving references by asking former supervisors for reference letters. Since these are usually glowing letters, however, most experienced interviewers don't rely on them as credible references for the very reason that they *are* so predictably favorable. After all, no applicant would circulate a reference letter if it were negative, so it wouldn't be prudent to take the positive ones seriously.

Of course, there are exceptions to this. You may find an interviewer who is impressed by letters you've attached to your resume and call you for an interview. Overall, though, you won't find them to be your key to a new job. The reality is that references of any type may contribute to an overall decision, but they are rarely the reason you are or are not hired.

LEGALITIES

Discrimination against applicants on the basis of race, sex, age, or religion, is of course illegal. Most interviewers are well trained to avoid it, but it's useful to have some basic knowledge of what interviewers can legally ask you in case you suspect you're being interviewed unfairly.

Most applications state something like ''Widget Corporation is an equal opportunity employer. We do not discriminate on the basis of sex, religion, color, race, age, national origin, physical handicap, or marital status.''

The chances of being asked a blatant question about this type of information are low, *unless* the person interviewing you has never heard of the civil rights movement! But you may be asked questions in a roundabout way in order to expose information about one of these hands-off topics.

Many people aren't at all offended by ''illegal'' questions. In fact, they're proud to talk about their spouse, church affiliation, or the like, which is their right. However, all applicants have the option *not* to reveal this information.

Some companies are anxious to know personal information about you. For example, they may feel (rightly or wrongly) that married employees are desirable because they have settled down or that employees who belong to a church have a greater sense of morality.

Larger companies, especially those with government contracts, often have quotas to fill. This means that a certain percentage of their employees *must* be minorities and/or protected groups (over a certain age, war veterans, etc.). If you happen to be a member of a minority, you may be looked upon as a more desirable candidate. However, you'll still need to have the necessary qualifications to be hired.

You should know that it's permissible for an employer to collect this kind of information as "post-hiring" data to be used for statistical purposes. Employers are encouraged to ask if you are willing to volunteer such information to help them comply with various state and federal requirements. You can volunteer the information when applying, or you can wait to see if you get hired and then answer the questions. The choice will be yours.

In the box that follows is a list of areas in which illegal questions might be asked in your interview. Read through them now, so that you can think about how you would react. Will you answer everything? Challenge the interviewer? Will you say you don't feel the questions are pertinent to filling the job? Will you be offended? Think through what your response would be if you were asked a direct question. Remember that such questions are generally not permissable, and that you have the right not to supply the information.

The following areas of personal information are considered hands-off for employers making hiring decisions. This is not a complete listing of such areas, but a sampling of some of the more general ones. State laws vary considerably on pre-employment discrimination laws. The laws that specifically prohibit discrimination are too long to list here.

Questions regarding your marital status, number and/or age of children or dependents, provisions for child care, or your maiden name.

Questions regarding pregnancy, childbearing, or birth control.

Name or address of your spouse, closest relatives, or children (emergency information excepted).

Questions that indicate with whom you reside.

Questions concerning your race or color.

Questions regarding your complexion or the color of your skin, eyes, or hair.

Questions regarding your birthplace or that of your parents or spouse.

Questions regarding your citizenship, nationality, or ancestry.*

Questions about your height and weight.

Requests that you attach a photograph of yourself to your application.

Questions regarding your general medical condition.

Questions regarding whether you have received Workers' Compensation.

Questions regarding your religion or the religious holidays you observe.

Questions concerned with whether or not you have a criminal record.

Questions regarding refusal or cancellation of bonding.

Questions regarding your military service (if any), including specific dates and type of discharge.

Questions regarding foreign military service.

Questions regarding your current or past assets, liabilities, or credit rating, including bankruptcy or garnishment.

Requests that you list the organizations, clubs, societies, and lodges to which you belong.

*With the 1987 signing of the Immigration Bill, it is permissible to ask, ''If you are not a U.S. citizen, do you have the right to work and remain in the United States?'' You will be expected to provide proof of citizenship or documentation of your right to work if hired.

On the other hand, otherwise unacceptable inquiries can be structured in a permissible way. For example, you can't be asked what your maiden name is. But you *can* be asked for any other names under which your school or work records have been filed. Employers are required to have work permits for minors under 18 and therefore must know their age. While they can't ask you the names and addresses of relatives, they will ask for the names and phone numbers of someone to contact in an emergency and they *may* ask what relation that person is to you. You might choose to use a relative as that contact. These examples show that the purpose of the questions and the way in which the questions are worded sometimes determine their appropriateness.

To sum up, your goal is to be hired, not to try to implicate companies in illegal discrimination. It's important to know what to expect and to think about how you'd react, but don't make a career out of this. If you go from interview to interview pointing fingers and claiming discrimination when you aren't hired, that history will eventually catch up with you. And, understandably, no one will want to hire you for fear you'll sue at the slightest provocation. Being prepared is essential; using the information as ammunition is *not*.

CONTACTS/NEPOTISM

Many employees have been hired over more qualified candidates because of who they know in the company. They may have personal contacts or even a relative in a position to influence the hiring process. If there's a family member or other contact who can help *you*, don't hesitate to ask. Of course, if you're the best-qualified candidate who missed the job because of nepotism (the hiring of relatives) or other favoritism, you'll probably feel it's unfair.

Whether you're the lucky or unlucky person in a situation like this, however, you should know that contacts and nepotism are commonly practiced in the job-hunting world. Should you be the favored one with the contact, it might help to know what approach an interviewer may have to take with you.

Many companies have policies about hiring relatives. The policy may forbid the hiring of family members if they will work in the same department or if one will supervise the other. Beyond that, it's quite common to hire relatives of current employees.

This can be uncomfortable for both you and the interviewer if you're the relative of an executive of the company. If you are the proverbial boss's nephew, for example, the interviewer may know that no matter what formalities are gone through for appearance's sake, you'll end up getting hired. Ironically, then, the interviewer will be under pressure to make an especially good impression on *you*, since you're a direct link to a person in charge.

Don't take advantage of this situation. You should treat the interview as you would if your uncle *weren't* the boss. From the start, you don't want your fellow employees to resent you. So treat the interviewer and anyone else you meet with respect. The recruiter will be left with a positive impression and you'll be off to the right start in your new job.

Put simply, use your contacts to your advantage, but don't abuse them. It will only hinder you later on.

INTERVIEWING THE INTERVIEWER

In a successful interview, the *applicant* always asks questions as well—both preplanned and spontaneous. The timing and content of these questions will be sure to figure in the ultimate evaluation of you. In fact, it's even appropriate to bring along a notepad with questions on it and to use it to jot down answers.

Even if everything you wanted to know is brought up in the course of conversation, still ask *something*, since it will be considered a sign of interest and analytic ability. It will also reinforce to the interviewer that you're not so desperate that you are willing to take the job without knowing all the details.

You'll have to make a judgment regarding the appropriateness of questions based on the type of interview you're having. The box that follows lists possible questions that are apropos to each type of interview. There are no hard and fast rules about this, and many questions apply to several different interview formats. Add questions of your own that are important to you and your situation.

If any of your questions lead to a response such as: "I'll let someone else answer that for you who is better qualified," don't be put off. The interviewer will be making the same type of judgment about the appropriateness of answering certain questions as you will have made to determine the appropriateness of asking those questions.

These questions are examples of those you might ask in a screening or selection interview. Add questions of your own, making sure they are suitable for that type of interview.

SCREENING INTERVIEWS

What direction is the company planning to take in the next year? Five years?

How long has the company been in business?

What growth has the company experienced?

Is there a probationary period? How long? What happens at the end of it?

Is this an exempt or nonexempt position? (See glossary at the end of this book for definitions.)

Will I be expected to supply my own tools, supplies, computer, and so on?

Is there compensation for overtime hours?

Who will make the final decision about hiring me?

Does the office have a smoking/nonsmoking policy? (This may be predetermined by a city ordinance.)

Is there an employees' credit union?

My questions: _____

_____

_____

_____

_____

_____

_____

SELECTION INTERVIEWS

What are the goals of this department? Are evaluations based on these goals?

What is the company's philosophy about internal promotion? Can you offer examples of people who have been promoted internally?

Who will I report to in this position? Will that person handle my reviews and evaluations?

Who will report to me (if anyone)?

Is there a defined job description? Is it one that I may be able to expand with time?

What will the training period be like?

My questions: _____

_____

_____

_____

_____

_____

_____

PERSONALITY AND CHEMISTRY

As frustrating and unfair as it can be, the fact is that all the preparation in the world won't help if the chemistry between you and your interviewer isn't right.

The dynamics need to work best between you and the person to whom you'll ultimately report, but you must get past other interviewers before you even meet that person. The chemistry needs to be right during the one or more interviews that take place along the way.

Unfortunately, this is an area that is out of your control. Everyone has experienced coming out of an interview knowing they're not going to get the job. When asked why they're so sure, they'll respond with such instinctive but generally accurate observations as, ''The chemistry was wrong,'' ''There were bad vibes,'' or ''I could tell we wouldn't get along.''

Interviewers may be left with the same impression. But good ones will refer you on anyway, if you have the right qualifications for the position. They'll overlook the personality barrier and realize you might mesh well with the potential supervisor. If you meet with interviewers who *can't* see beyond their own personalities, you're unfortunately out of luck.

It can be extremely frustrating to have this experience with a recruiter or anyone in the first stages of interviewing. Conversely, if you've just met with your potential supervisor and leave feeling this way, it may be a blessing. Your instincts might be telling you this isn't a person you could work with day after day, and you may be better off not starting the job in the first place.

Another frustration can occur when you meet with interviewers who are so seasoned that they're able to maintain a polite and pleasant rapport throughout your meeting, even if they've already decided not to recommend you. In all likelihood, they'll smile, continue asking and answering questions, and shake your hand so assuredly that you'll leave feeling confident you passed the screening. You are completely unprepared to find out later that the job went to someone else. Remember that interviewers are trained to be friendly and receptive to *all* applicants. Don't assume that, just because you got along well in the interview, you'll automatically get hired.

Some positions actually require a certain type of personality (although this could never be advertised or overtly discussed). An example might be one in which someone will constantly be greeting the public. This requires an employee with a cheerful disposition, animated personality, and infectious warmth. If you're applying for this type of job, but mention in the interview that you're happiest working alone and are uncomfortable around a lot of people (*not* exactly the thing to say under the circumstances, of course), the interviewer may disqualify you immediately.

The best way to avoid this is to act natural and be—here's that word again—honest. Think about what personality traits will be called for and whether you're suited to that position. If it seems right for you and you're able to convey that fact during the interview, you'll make a favorable impression.

Consciously or not, the interviewer will make determinations about your personality and of the chemistry between you. Personality and chemistry inevitably influence the interviewer's evaluation. If you don't have great chemistry with your interviewer, all you can do is hope that more tangible matters such as your job experiences and education will be given more weight than how well you hit it off.

REACHING A DECISION

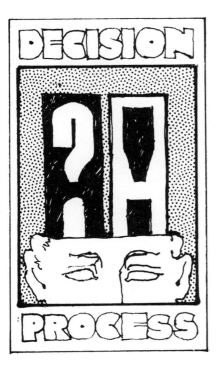

At what point do interviewers make up their mind about a candidate? Many say that when someone is wrong for the job, they know within the first five minutes and any further discussion is simply a formality. In the majority of cases, this is how applicants are screened out. However, when an applicant is *right* for the job, the decision is rarely made that quickly.

The best applicant is chosen based on consideration of the information gathered during all the interviews and listed on applications, from references (in some cases), and portfolios or clippings (if submitted). Many interviewers draw a two-column table with the positives listed down one side and negatives listed down the other. This gives them a visual representation of all the considerations going through their minds. Nevertheless, quick decisions sometimes are made, and this is unfortunately out of your control as well.

Seasoned interviewers fairly weigh an applicant's strengths and weaknesses. They keep their biases out of the decision-making process and consider every individual they've met for the position. Hopefully, this is the type of interviewer you'll meet.

FOR STUDENTS AND RECENT COLLEGE GRADUATES ONLY

If you're a student or recent college graduate, you needn't feel disadvantaged just because you may lack the experience in a full-time job. Potential employers realize you haven't yet had the opportunity to put your just-acquired knowledge and skills to use. However, don't underestimate the experience, which may or may not be directly job-related, that you *have* had. Add it to your resumé and discuss it in your interviews.

Most significantly, *any* job that you're holding now or held as a student is meaningful, sometimes for reasons that aren't obvious. Along those lines, if you graduate from college with a B average, you can demonstrate that you are the best candidate if, for example, you worked 20 hours a week over those four years as a cashier at the college bookstore. Of course, the experience gained working in that position probably won't have an obvious relationship to the one you are now applying for. However, a closer look at this previous job could provide an astute interviewer with quite a bit of insight.

First, there are certain key personality traits that could immediately be inferred. In particular, your ability to maintain a good grade point average while working 20 hours a week would suggest that you're a disciplined and organized person who was able to arrange a productive work/study schedule. Also, the fact that you held the same position for four years would indicate tenacity, honesty, and reliability.

Secondly, there are specific skills you would likely have learned in your college job that could be helpful to a potential employer, including a mathematical savvy, an ability to use business machines, and a flair for relating to customers.

An experienced interviewer would think about all of these things, but a measure of prodding on your part couldn't hurt. If you feel an interviewer is ignoring your prior work experience and failing to grasp the full range of your professional *and* personal attributes, by all means state your case at a natural point in the conversation (without indulging in egomania, naturally).

The example of a cashier in a bookstore was used because both interviewers and young applicants themselves may write off a previous job of this kind as worthless. As you've seen, though, it should be presented as an indicator of your potential value as an employee.

Since there *are* so many work experiences that can be regarded as meaningful by employers, then, maximize your chances by adding to your resumé virtually any jobs you've had as a student, whether on summer or semester breaks or during a regular school period. You'll be showing an interviewer that instead of using free time to lie in the sun, you chose to go to work, make money, and gain experience. You may have in reality done it just to earn a few dollars, but even *that* will probably be perceived as evidence of a disciplined and serious individual.

Another good resumé item for students are internships done either over a summer break or during the school year. Many interviewers are aware of the heavy competition there is for good internships. You may therefore even get credit in their minds for having *tried* to land an internship, so don't forget to mention any such attempts, as well as why you may have been passed over.

Many students apply for a specific internship because it's directly related to the field they've chosen. If this is the case, your internship experience is especially valuable, and you should use the interview to explain what you learned and how it enhances you as a candidate.

Other experiences interviewers find valuable are extracurricular school activities. These include on-campus clubs, sports-related and student government activities, sororities, and fraternaties. Membership alone won't be considered noteworthy, since most students get involved in one or more such groups during their college years. You can make membership count if you can show that participation in these activities helped you learn more about organization or management or maybe more about yourself.

For instance, two years of playing intramural soccer may not be impressive on its own. However, if you organized the team, were responsible for scheduling practices, ordered uniforms and trophies, and had a winning team, you'll have something to talk about. Needless to say, it will be even more impressive if the skills you acquired are related to the position in question. If the applicant in the above example were applying for a management training program, his or her experience in something as simple as soccer could therefore be very impressive since it would demonstrate a track record in organizing, scheduling, and winning!

Many students feel intimidated by the interviewing process itself. Larger corporations tend to do college recruiting on campus if the school has a well-organized placement center. For many students, this makes the ordeal more relaxed because they are in familiar surroundings, perhaps with their friends being interviewed in the very next room. However, it's essential to approach an on-campus interview as if you're in an office and to dress accordingly.

Remember that the people you're going to meet know that you are a student and understand why your resumé is short and your style possibly not yet polished. With well trained interviewers, these factors won't be held against you.

Recent graduates sometimes make their biggest mistakes by exaggerating or lying about experience, grades, and classes taken—information that is easily verified once you're hired, at which time you may be asked to sign a consent form so that the company can request it from your college.

Avoid being overly eager and taking the I'll-do-anything approach. If you're unfocused about your career and don't care what you fall into, this strategy may work for you. However, if you've chosen your career goals, it may take more time and more interviews, but you'll be more likely to get what you want in the end. Listen carefully, don't give lengthy or nebulous answers, don't ask questions about salary too soon, and be sure to ask key questions about available positions.

You can avoid interview pitfalls by knowing what you want to say (without over-rehearsing), considering your career goals, and—as usual—relaxing!

POST-INTERVIEW

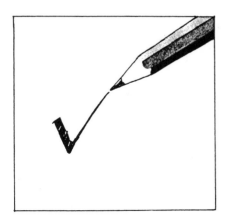

Immediately after an interview, send a thank-you letter to each person you met with, being sure to spell all names properly and to use correct titles.

It's advisable to send a letter even if you're not really interested in the position. You may apply with the same company again in the future or be referred to another opening.

Thank-you letters should be sent for every type of interview, although the content varies slightly. For a screening or selection interview, thank the individual for meeting with you and describing the position to you. Express your interest in the position and your desire to work for the company.

If you had an exploratory interview and no specific position was discussed (this may be true of a screening interview as well), thank them for their time and ask to be kept in mind should the right opening come along.

Avoid using the thank-you letter as another opportunity to explain your qualifications. The letter should be short and concise.

> ◆**TIP:** When you print your resumé, purchase extra matching blank paper to use for your thank-you letters and any other correspondence. When your resumé and correspondence is pulled from the files, it will look like one complete, neat package.

Usually, you'll be told to expect a letter or phone call within a certain amount of time, letting you know whether or not you got the job. Aside from your thank-you note, it's best not to contact the company during this period. There are several factors that may delay a company's decision, and you must abide by its time frame. This can be a real nail-biting time, but you'll have to wait it out. If the designated time goes by and you still haven't heard anything, you may call to ask when the decision will be reached.

If you receive a rejection letter or phone call, it is perfectly acceptable to contact the interviewer and ask that you be considered for future positions. It is a bad idea, however, to call if you're going to be surly and demand to know why you weren't chosen. This may easily anger the recruiter and ruin your chances of *ever* working there.

One tactic many applicants use after an interview is to call before they've heard anything to say they have an offer from another company and need an answer right away. However, there's no way of predicting whether this will work in your favor. If the company wants you badly enough, it may be pressured into making a quick decision and hiring you; but if you're a borderline candidate, this technique may have no effect. So many candidates have tried it that some interviewers ignore their plea for a quick decision. Others have the attitude that the candidate needs to decide which company he or she would rather work for and are willing to wait for the decision. If you try to bluff your way in, it very well may not work.

If it's true that you have another offer, you may be asked for details such as the position in question, the salary, benefits, and so on. The company may start a bidding war for you and offer you more or better perks. On the other hand, it may congratulate you and move on to another applicant.

For some people, the time after an interview is far worse than any other time involved in job hunting. Sitting by the phone makes the day seem longer, and as each day goes by your hopes diminish. Remember that the people that interviewed you are busy and may be recruiting for other positions besides the one you're interested in. You never want to appear over-anxious, so you'll simply have to sit tight, wait, and hope to hear some good news.

DO'S (AND DON'TS) FOR INTERVIEWING

Trying to remember all the do's and don'ts, shoulds and shouldn'ts would be impossible. Refer to this list before each interview for quick reminders of the most vital things to remember. They have all been written in the positive DO, so just turn them around and you'll know the don'ts.

DO research the position, company or field.

DO practice interviews with a friend to ease your nervousness and pinpoint undesirable habits.

DO ask for directions and parking instructions.

DO give yourself ample time for the interview.

DO try to arrange the interview when you won't have to worry about the time you're spending.

DO confirm your appointment ahead of time.

DO arrive alone, without bringing a friend or family member with you.

DO arrive early.

DO be prepared with names and addresses of references.

DO prepare your references for receiving a call.

DO take advantage of any and all contacts, including family members.

DO use contacts to supply you with information.

DO understand the different types of interviews so that you'll know what to expect from each one.

DO have ideas about salary before the meeting.

DO overdress rather than underdress.

DO'S AND DON'TS
FOR INTERVIEWING (Continued)

DO treat the receptionist or secretary with respect.

DO remember everyone's names and correct titles.

DO complete the application or any forms given to you.

DO make eye contact.

DO give answers that are concise and relevant.

DO ask questions of the interviewer.

DO allow the interviewer to guide the conversation.

DO tell the truth and exaggerate *only* if you can back it up.

DO avoid pat and cliché-ridden answers.

DO try to appear selective, even if you're over-anxious.

DO be prepared to discuss your former employers, even if the experience was negative.

DO be prepared if you're interviewing for a position where there's little room for salary negotiation.

DO ask about specific benefits you're interested in.

DO use benefits as a negotiating tool when possible.

DO mention work experience and extracurricular activities while in college (especially recent graduates).

DO follow up with a thank-you letter.

Most importantly, DO everything you can to appear and *be* relaxed!

CONCLUSION

Use this book as a reference tool before to your interviews, but don't let it stop at that. Build your own interviewing book, including comments about your most *and* least successful interviews, as well as lists of the kinds of information you need to ask for, benefits you regard as essential, questions you want to ask, and virtually anything and everything you consider meaningful. Keep a thorough account of all your interviewers and the contacts you make along the way, noting their exact affiliations and titles.

Whatever twists and turns your career takes as you go along, you *will* eventually land the job you want. And though you may at the time attribute getting that job primarily to good luck and good timing, chances are it will have stemmed directly from the impact you made in your interview.

Remember that interviewing is a skill that can be practiced, perfected, and used to tremendous advantage, time and time again. Practice and perfect the necessary skills whenever possible, and very soon the most difficult ''job'' you'll be facing is deciding which offer to accept.

TOOLS OF THE TRADE

The checklist below is to help you remember all the essential elements you'll need before and after an interview. Although all of these are mentioned elsewhere in this book, this compilation will help you remember things that you might otherwise forget during this busy time. A quick glance prior to each interview will assure your readiness before and after your meetings.

1. Driving and parking instructions _____

2. Name of person(s) you'll be meeting _____

3. Resume and matching paper _____

4. Cover letters _____

5. Portfolio, writing samples (if appropriate) _____

6. Reference list _____

7. Salary information _____

8. Information & questions about the company _____

9. Your business cards (if appropriate) _____

10. Business cards of those you meet _____

11. Thank you letters _____

12. Correct phone numbers (yours and theirs) _____

GLOSSARY

Affirmative Action. A corporation's pro-active efforts to promote the hiring of minorities and protected groups. A company can be required by state and federal agencies to implement an affirmative action program.

Age Discrimination Act. Prohibits discrimination on the basis of age when individuals are at least 40 but less than 70 years of age.

Applicant flow data. Data that is collected for record keeping and statistical purposes. It may be requested as voluntary information before hiring in order to comply with federal and state requirements and to support affirmative action.

At-will employment. Employment that is for no definite period of time and that may be terminated at any time without prior notice. It assumes that termination is for cause and that progressive discipline was used. Does not apply when there is an employment contract signed by both parties.

EEOC (Equal Employment Opportunity Commission). A body of the federal government that was created under Title IV of the Civil Rights Act. Among other things, it requires employers to develop hiring practices and policies that adhere to nondiscriminatory selection practices.

Equal Pay Act. Bars sex discrimination in pay when jobs are equivalent.

Exempt employee. Generally, exempt employees receive compensation on a salary basis and devote a majority of time to managerial duties or assisting in managerial duties. (Often further categorized in the subgroups of executive, administrative, professional, and sales).

Immigration Reform and Control Act of 1986. The Immigration and Naturalization Service's strict rules, which define an employer's responsibility to avoid knowingly hiring illegal aliens.

MBO (Management by objectives). Method of evaluating performance; the employee and supervisor develop objectives and assess performance against each.

Minimum wage. The minimum hourly wage that employers must pay. The rate is regulated by the Industrial Welfare Commission. Employees who customarily receive tips are excepted.

Non-exempt employee. Generally, one that receives compensation based on an hourly calculation. Punches time clock or completes time card. Generally has no managerial duties and is eligible for overtime.

Probation period. Period established by employer after which new employees are evaluated. New employees are rarely eligible for benefits before their probation ends. During their probation period, employees can be terminated without cause.

Progressive discipline. A sequence of disciplinary actions, beginning with a friendly warning and ending with a statement that the employee will be fired if certain conditions are not met. The employer notifies an employee that his or her work performance is not satisfactory and what standards must be met. This is usually done in written communication so that the employee is clear about what to do, and the company has a record of action taken.

Termination for cause. Termination of employment for reasons widely recognized as appropriate—for example, failure to meet minimal job requirements, drunkenness on the job, or sexual harrassment of subordinates.

Union. Bargaining group representing employees in an agreement entered into with the company (management). The agreement outlines which specific positions are governed by the union rules and the wage scales and rights of those employees.

Union job. One that is governed by the union bargaining unit.

NOTES

FOR OTHER FIFTY-MINUTE SELF-STUDY BOOKS
SEE ORDER FORM AT THE BACK OF THE BOOK.

NOTES

FOR OTHER FIFTY-MINUTE SELF-STUDY BOOKS
SEE ORDER FORM AT THE BACK OF THE BOOK.

THE FIFTY-MINUTE SERIES

Quantity	Title	Code #	Price	Amount
	MANAGEMENT TRAINING			
	Self-Managing Teams	000-0	$7.95	
	Delegating For Results	008-6	$7.95	
	Successful Negotiation—Revised	09-2	$7.95	
	Increasing Employee Productivity	010-8	$7.95	
	Personal Performance Contracts—Revised	12-2	$7.95	
	Team Building—Revised	16-5	$7.95	
	Effective Meeting Skills	33-5	$7.95	
	An Honest Day's Work: Motivating Employees To Excel	39-4	$7.95	
	Managing Disagreement Constructively	41-6	$7.95	
	Training Managers To Train	43-2	$7.95	
	Learning To Lead	043-4	$7.95	
	The Fifty-Minute Supervisor—Revised	58-0	$7.95	
	Leadership Skills For Women	62-9	$7.95	
	Systematic Problem Solving & Decision Making	63-7	$7.95	
	Coaching & Counseling	68-8	$7.95	
	Ethics In Business	69-6	$7.95	
	Understanding Organizational Change	71-8	$7.95	
	Project Management	75-0	$7.95	
	Risk Taking	76-9	$7.95	
	Managing Organizational Change	80-7	$7.95	
	Working Together In A Multi-Cultural Organization	85-8	$7.95	
	Selecting And Working With Consultants	87-4	$7.95	
	PERSONNEL MANAGEMENT			
	Your First Thirty Days: A Professional Image in a New Job	003-5	$7.95	
	Office Management: A Guide To Productivity	005-1	$7.95	
	Men and Women: Partners at Work	009-4	$7.95	
	Effective Performance Appraisals—Revised	11-4	$7.95	
	Quality Interviewing—Revised	13-0	$7.95	
	Personal Counseling	14-9	$7.95	
	Attacking Absenteeism	042-6	$7.95	
	New Employee Orientation	46-7	$7.95	
	Professional Excellence For Secretaries	52-1	$7.95	
	Guide To Affirmative Action	54-8	$7.95	
	Writing A Human Resources Manual	70-X	$7.95	
	Winning at Human Relations	86-6	$7.95	
	WELLNESS			
	Mental Fitness	15-7	$7.95	
	Wellness in the Workplace	020-5	$7.95	
	Personal Wellness	021-3	$7.95	

THE FIFTY-MINUTE SERIES (Continued)

Quantity	Title	Code #	Price	Amount
	WELLNESS (CONTINUED)			
	Preventing Job Burnout	23-8	$7.95	
	Job Performance and Chemical Dependency	27-0	$7.95	
	Overcoming Anxiety	029-9	$7.95	
	Productivity at the Workstation	041-8	$7.95	
	COMMUNICATIONS			
	Technical Writing In The Corporate World	004-3	$7.95	
	Giving and Receiving Criticism	023-X	$7.95	
	Effective Presentation Skills	24-6	$7.95	
	Better Business Writing—Revised	25-4	$7.95	
	Business Etiquette And Professionalism	032-9	$7.95	
	The Business Of Listening	34-3	$7.95	
	Writing Fitness	35-1	$7.95	
	The Art Of Communicating	45-9	$7.95	
	Technical Presentation Skills	55-6	$7.95	
	Making Humor Work	61-0	$7.95	
	Visual Aids In Business	77-7	$7.95	
	Speed-Reading In Business	78-5	$7.95	
	Publicity Power	82-3	$7.95	
	Influencing Others	84-X	$7.95	
	SELF-MANAGEMENT			
	Attitude: Your Most Priceless Possession-Revised	011-6	$7.95	
	Personal Time Management	22-X	$7.95	
	Successful Self-Management	26-2	$7.95	
	Balancing Home And Career—Revised	035-3	$7.95	
	Developing Positive Assertiveness	38-6	$7.95	
	The Telephone And Time Management	53-X	$7.95	
	Memory Skills In Business	56-4	$7.95	
	Developing Self-Esteem	66-1	$7.95	
	Creativity In Business	67-X	$7.95	
	Managing Personal Change	74-2	$7.95	
	Stop Procrastinating: Get To Work!	88-2	$7.95	
	CUSTOMER SERVICE/SALES TRAINING			
	Sales Training Basics—Revised	02-5	$7.95	
	Restaurant Server's Guide—Revised	08-4	$7.95	
	Telephone Courtesy And Customer Service	18-1	$7.95	
	Effective Sales Management	031-0	$7.95	
	Professional Selling	42-4	$7.95	
	Customer Satisfaction	57-2	$7.95	
	Telemarketing Basics	60-2	$7.95	
	Calming Upset Customers	65-3	$7.95	
	Quality At Work	72-6	$7.95	
	Managing Quality Customer Service	83-1	$7.95	
	Quality Customer Service—Revised	95-5	$7.95	
	SMALL BUSINESS AND FINANCIAL PLANNING			
	Understanding Financial Statements	022-1	$7.95	
	Marketing Your Consulting Or Professional Services	40-8	$7.95	

THE FIFTY-MINUTE SERIES (Continued)

Quantity	Title	Code #	Price	Amount
	SMALL BUSINESS AND FINANCIAL PLANNING (CONTINUED)			
	Starting Your New Business	44-0	$7.95	
	Personal Financial Fitness—Revised	89-0	$7.95	
	Financial Planning With Employee Benefits	90-4	$7.95	
	BASIC LEARNING SKILLS			
	Returning To Learning: Getting Your G.E.D.	002-7	$7.95	
	Study Skills Strategies—Revised	05-X	$7.95	
	The College Experience	007-8	$7.95	
	Basic Business Math	024-8	$7.95	
	Becoming An Effective Tutor	028-0	$7.95	
	CAREER PLANNING			
	Career Discovery	07-6	$7.95	
	Effective Networking	030-2	$7.95	
	Preparing for Your Interview	033-7	$7.95	
	Plan B: Protecting Your Career	48-3	$7.95	
	I Got the Job!	59-9	$7.95	
	RETIREMENT			
	Personal Financial Fitness—Revised	89-0	$7.95	
	Financial Planning With Employee Benefits	90-4	$7.95	

OTHER CRISP INC. BOOKS

Quantity	Title	Code #	Price	Amount
	Desktop Publishing	001-9	$ 5.95	
	Stepping Up To Supervisor	11-8	$13.95	
	The Unfinished Business Of Living: Helping Aging Parents	19-X	$12.95	
	Managing Performance	23-7	$19.95	
	Be True To Your Future: A Guide To Life Planning	47-5	$13.95	
	Up Your Productivity	49-1	$10.95	
	Comfort Zones: Planning Your Future 2/e	73-4	$13.95	
	Copyediting 2/e	94-7	$18.95	
	Recharge Your Career	027-2	$12.95	
	Practical Time Management	275-4	$13.95	

VIDEO TITLE*

Quantity	Video Title*	Code #	Preview	Purchase	Amount
	Attitude: Your Most Priceless Possession	012-4	$25.00	$395.00	
	Quality Customer Service	013-2	$25.00	$395.00	
	Team Building	014-2	$25.00	$395.00	
	Job Performance & Chemical Dependency	015-9	$25.00	$395.00	
	Better Business Writing	016-7	$25.00	$395.00	
	Comfort Zones	025-6	$25.00	$395.00	
	Creativity in Business	036-1	$25.00	$395.00	
	Motivating at Work	037-X	$25.00	$395.00	
	Calming Upset Customers	040-X	$25.00	$395.00	
	Balancing Home and Career	048-5	$25.00	$395.00	
	Stress and Mental Fitness	049-3	$25.00	$395.00	

(*Note: All tapes are VHS format. Video package includes five books and a Leader's Guide.)

THE FIFTY-MINUTE SERIES
(Continued)

	Amount
Total Books	
Less Discount (5 or more different books 20% sampler)	
Total Videos	
Less Discount (purchase of 3 or more videos earn 20%)	
Shipping ($3.50 per video, $.50 per book)	
California Tax (California residents add 7%)	
TOTAL	

☐ Send volume discount information.

☐ Please charge the following credit card

☐ Please send me a catalog.

☐ Mastercard   ☐ VISA   ☐ AMEX

Account No. _____   Name (as appears on card) _____

Ship to: _____   Bill to: _____

_____   _____

_____   _____

_____   _____

Phone number: _____   P.O. # _____

**All orders except those with a P.O.# must be prepaid.
For more information Call (415) 949-4888 or FAX (415) 949-1610.**

BUSINESS REPLY
FIRST CLASS   PERMIT NO. 884   LOS ALTOS, CA

POSTAGE WILL BE PAID BY ADDRESSEE

Crisp Publications, Inc.
95 First Street
Los Altos, CA 94022

NO POSTAGE
NECESSARY
IF MAILED
IN THE
UNITED STATES

2611